From Within the Hidden Places

Tracey Lafayette

authorHOUSE®

AuthorHouse™ UK Ltd.
500 Avebury Boulevard
Central Milton Keynes, MK9 2BE
www.authorhouse.co.uk
Phone: 08001974150

© *2009 Tracey Lafayette. All rights reserved.*

No part of this book may be reproduced, stored in a retrieval system, or transmitted by any means without the written permission of the author.

First published by AuthorHouse 12/17/2009

ISBN: 978-1-4490-4995-9 (sc)

The NIV Text maybe quoted in any from, scripture taken from the Holy Bible, New International Version, Copyright 1973,1978,1984 By International Bible Society, use by permission of Zondervan all rights reserved.

NIV Women of faith Study Bible, New International Version Copyright 2001 By Zondervan all rights reserved.

The Message Remix the Bible in contemporary language Copyright 2003 By Eugene H Peterson all rights reserved.

Verses marked TLB taken from The Living Bible Copyright 1971 used by permission of Tyndale House Publishers Inc, Wheaton Illinois 60189, all rights reserved.

Scripture quotations marked HCSB have been taken from The Holman Christian Standard Bible copyright 1999,2002,2003 By Holman Bible Publishers, used by permission.

The poems in this book about Death and Air were written by Tracey Linda Lafayette Copyright 2009

This book is printed on acid-free paper.

About the Author

Tracey Linda Lafayette was born in London in 1968 and has three sisters. She studied at Clissold Park School in Stoke Newington and became a chef at the age of 18. After 22 years in the profession, she decided to go into youth work and currently works with families and young children.

Acknowledgements

I would like to thank my family and the people that have been close to me at this time. To my sister Denise on her contribution to the Beautiful Game section. Thank you so much. I would also like to give thanks to the Lord Jesus Christ who continues to strengthen in love and great faith. I appreciate this so, so much.
Many thanks.

Tracey xx

Be alert, be present. I am about to do something brand-new. It's bursting out! Don't you see it? There it is! I'm making a road through the desert, rivers in the badlands. (Isaiah 43:19 the Message)

The earth is the Lord's and all its fullness, the world and those who dwell therein, For He has founded it upon the seas, And established it upon the waters. (Psalm 23: 1-2 NKJV)

Food and Diet

Food is nourishing both to our bodies and our souls. To some people it can be seen as a comforter, helps lift our spirits, and can even relieve us in the most traumatic of circumstances. Some foods such as fruit for instance can even cleanse our bodies so that it can function properly. Having worked as a chef I know what it is like to prepare food. It is usually a long process, but the end result can be a satisfying one. In some cases after eating a nice meal we may sometimes feel well rested or may end up falling asleep.

On the other hand we can at times complex food in terms of how we prepare and treat it. Some people even get into arguments about food; in the catering industry for example, the behaviour of some chefs to go above and beyond to perfect creation in their meals has led to moments of verbal outbursts and altercations.

Why does this happen we may ask ourselves? This is because some people may have different ideas as to the way the food is prepared and made according to their particular taste. In some restaurants the food is also prepared according to its reputation (if it serves haute cuisine meals, has a Michelin award status or caters to those who are influential), and because of this high demand it can sometimes further complex matters.

Because food is a source of life some chefs in the catering industry hold themselves up in high esteem, as they believe that they are creating something from nothing and perhaps see themselves as "god-like" in terms of status.

The book of Genesis 1:1(NIV) describes God's plans of putting heaven and earth into being: In the beginning God created the heavens and the earth. The earth was formless and empty. Food is also like this before it is prepared – formless and empty.

Food in the spirit sense is the Bible - the Word of God. It is up to us as individuals to be aware of this or not or want to believe or disbelieve it. The Word, be it spoken in prayer or by reading it is very nourishing to both our souls and spirit.

As I mentioned earlier when we eat food and it is satisfying we may sometimes fall asleep because the food has given us comfort. The same thing happens with the Word of God. When reading the Bible we feel rested and comforted because of the prayer that is digested into our souls. The Psalmist writes, Oh, taste and see that the Lord is good; Blessed is the man who trusts in Him! (Psalm 34:8 NKJV)

The Word of God in the spiritual sense is food. The Bible also describes Jesus as the bread of life. "I am the bread of life," Jesus told them. "No one who comes to Me will ever be hungry, and no one who believes in Me will ever be thirsty again." (John 6:35 HCSB)

Whatever we eat these days we may sometimes hear of reports from experts saying that some foods are good for us while some foods are bad, therefore we should avoid them. Because they are experts we sometimes believe this to be true because the heart and mind is working in one accord.

When I look at the pomegranate fruit I personally think that it looks like the heart organ; the juice from the pomegranate also contains a good source of vitamins. There are unfortunately some foods that can cause us health problems or even kill us if we consume too much of it. Food is spirit which is why when we eat the right foods it can have an uplifting effect. If we have eaten a good meal we may say, "Oh that hit the spot," and in this case the spot is the Holy Spirit.

When food is consumed it breaks down into our spirit. But there are some foods that trigger allergies and can cause some people to have a severe reaction if it stays in the body and affects the system from within. The Word of God, which is the food in the spirit sense, does not do this; instead it comforts us so that we can have the right reaction.

God/Columbo (Just One More Thing)

In the TV series *Columbo*, the detective always knew who the murderer was and in many ways could be compared to how God is perceived and how he sees things before they happen. The character of Columbo was seen as bumbling and not tidy in appearance, however he was also shown to be humble and simple.

Some people in this world may also see God as a Columbo type character and when things seem to go wrong he is seen as bumbling and missing the point. Columbo was anything but simple minded, and was spot on as God is.

Columbo was not only a clever detective but also very humble in his approach when working on a case. His distinguished attire was a shabby rain Mack which appeared throughout the course of the TV series and feature-length TV movies.

In *Columbo* the person who committed the murder believed that they had carried out the perfect crime, had carefully covered their tracks, and could outsmart him because they underestimated him in terms of his persona and dress sense.

In spite of this Columbo always had a knack of coming back time after time to the murder suspect with more questions and theories and before he finished his enquiries he would turn to them and say, "Just one more thing." I feel that some people may believe that God does not know what is going on and does not see anything.

But the Bible says that God sees and knows everything. He knows about everyone, everywhere. Everything about us is bare and wide open to the all seeing eyes of our living God. Nothing can be hidden from Him to whom we must explain all that we have done. (Hebrews 4:13 TLB)

We therefore have to be careful in what we do and say. When Columbo was hot on the trail of the murderer he would always show up unexpectedly and actually irritate the murderer with his theories. By doing this his mere presence began to convict them. In an episode of *Columbo* called *Blueprint for Murder (*1972), the murderer actually calls Columbo "the omnipresent detective." What does omnipresent mean one may ask? Omnipresent means all knowing and all seeing. Only God is omnipresent, has the power to convict people, and can predict what has already happened previously.

The Beautiful Game or is it? (Part One)

Football is the number one sport around the world and many have adopted this as the new religion in their lives. Some might say that the chairman of football clubs could be likened to God in that the chairman is the head, they delegate tasks to the manager, and in some cases even the players. Their decision is final and they may sometimes bring about fear amongst the people (they have the power to hire and fire managers, may buy top players to keep supporters on their side or if they lose interest in the club could pull out their investment all together).

The managers could be compared to the church ministers in that they influence the players whereas the minister will influence the congregation. If you look at Sir Alex Ferguson, the manager of Manchester United, it can be said that he is a highly influential leader. Over the years he has helped the club win numerous trophies and in 1999 managed the team to win the English Premier League, FA Cup and European Champions League all in the same season, a feat which has not yet been replicated by another English team.

He is also a manager who expects the very best from his players and his tough no nonsense approach to management has earned him the respect of United players both past and present as well as rival managers. If you have a good church minister in charge, they too can bring about a good atmosphere in the congregation in that people will want to proudly engage in church activities, be firm supporters of their church and be inspired by God's Word.

God (The Boss)

The boss of this particular company employs many people in his organization and he is fair in all his ways. Sometimes it is his employees who think that they are above their station and know everything, and may try to change things to suit their needs.

The boss gives you a choice as to whether you want to work for him or not and is very patient. The work has to be of a high quality and excellence otherwise another person may be appointed in your position. The wages (the rewards from God) are unbelievable and the atmosphere is great; some of the other staff appointed by God can be friendly and helpful while others sometimes can become envious of your position.

Jesus (The Company)

If Jesus were a company then it would be fair to say that his business would be the only one that would not go into liquidation. Jesus Christ is the same yesterday, today and forever. (Hebrews 13:8 NIV)

His boss (God) is highly intelligent and is always on top of things and although his workers may leave when the work gets tough, there are always new recruits waiting in the wings, and he never forgets an old employee who is willing not only to serve his company but others also. For God is not unjust; He will not forget your work and the love you showed for His name when you served the saints – and you continue to serve them. (Hebrews 6:10 HCSB)

Sometimes there are other businesses that will check out the company accounts of Jesus (the Bible) and for this they can be quite critical, but his accounts always seem to be on their lips, even to the point that some will want to find fault, some will just be looking out of curiosity, while others who were maybe scathing in the beginning may find themselves joining his company.

His company has been going for donkey's years (pardon the pun) and is a place where the boss knows everybody's names, their talents and where they live. Everyone in the business is treated as equals as there are no favourites. Paul writes in Romans 2:1(NIV): There is no favouritism with God. There are some people within the company that will try to exploit the name of Jesus by motioning a vote of no confidence against him as they believe that they can actually run his company better.

In some cases these people will try to discredit Jesus' name with their reckless actions, but everything that is done to destabilise his company will be exposed as the actions of Jesus is not underhand, and those who do not follow his ways will eventually come to the realization that their services are no longer be required (in other words, you need to shape up or ship out).

The Company Policy

If you work for a company where you interact with the public there are signs displayed within that organization informing members of the public that any physical or verbal abuse made by them towards a worker will not be tolerated and that the company has the right to take the strictest course of action to deal with such matters.

When we read such policies we may think that this only

applies to the public and may not realise that physical and verbal abuse can also occur between staff members within a company and should therefore not be hidden because it is an in-house matter. What we may also find is that a lot of abuse and bullying takes place in certain organisations and companies, yet this could be overlooked because we sometimes look at the outsider causing the problems and not those from within.

The Bible is a policy for believing Christians and teaches them the ways in which to conduct their lives. However, there are some people who think that the Bible is a warning for outsiders and not for those within.

The Company Takeover

Some leaders these days may sometimes misuse their position of authority. Leaders are supposed to meet the people where they are at and guide them. In the beginning when God created Adam and Eve, Adam being created first by God was given leadership over Eve; firstly God had leadership over Adam. The leaders these days have to respect the helpers that they are given.

Eve was Adam's helper; however she was misled by the wrong company (the devil/serpent) who came to her. The serpent said to the Woman: "You won't die. God knows that the moment you eat from that tree, you'll see what's really going on. You'll be like God, knowing everything, ranging all the way from good to evil." (Genesis 3:4-5 the Message)

To paraphrase the above scripture: "I have this offer for you, it's very rewarding and in return you'll be the boss of own company and you'll be able to set your own rules." But what was Adam doing for this to happen? Was he not looking out for his helper?

Some leaders today are not looking out for their workers/helpers in the proper manner. When Eve was approached by the wrong company, the true company (God) questioned Adam about their decision to join the wrong company. Adam then blamed Eve for her lack of decision: "The Man said, "The Woman you gave me as a companion, she gave me fruit from the tree, and, yes, I ate it." (Genesis 3:12 the Message)

In other words, Adam, who was supposed to be in charge of Eve, shifted the blame unto her. When some leaders don't do their job properly they are quick to blame their workers or helpers yet fail to recognize that they have been given a position of leadership which is important.

God (The Surgeon)

God's deliverance is to get rid of the things that hold you back (the spiritual element of things that will prevent a person from moving on). It reminds me of when people go to the hospital or have an appointment with the doctor. After confessing to the doctor their symptoms and ailments, the doctor can then decide the procedure to make them better.

Before this can happen the doctor needs to run some tests or carry out some x-rays examinations to get to the root of the problem and identify it; with some symptoms it may take a little longer to process depending on the ailment.

Once the tests and x-rays have been given the all clear the patient is now ready for surgery/deliverance. In the operating theatre the lead surgeon/Jesus, who is the master physician is assisted by his nurses/helpers. During the surgery/prayers, the surgeon/Jesus is able to proceed by cutting away the ailments, which are the issues of life affecting the person and the body.

After the surgery is completed there is a period of recovery and a restoration process needs to be applied to assist with the healing. From a biblical viewpoint it means being thankful to the Lord at all times. O Lord my God, I will give thanks to You forever. (Psalm 30: 12 NKJV)

Foundations
It makes you think...

Everything needs a foundation otherwise without it how can you build anything? When make-up is applied the foundation is put on first and then (depending on the steps taken) the blusher eyeliner and mascara should follow. Without foundation a house or property, wherever you are building it will not be able to stand firm and will fall. A tree stands because of the foundation that is rooted deeply in the soil. Relationships and friendships are like this and need to be recognized as foundations otherwise the slightest shift or disagreement may cause it to fall apart.

ISSUES, ISSUES, READ ALL ABOUT IT!

As human beings we may at times make a small thing into a big issue. Everything is simple but we may complex it or put our spin on it, therefore making it complicated and difficult to understand. The Gospel Message as told by Christ himself is so simple that even a child can understand it.

When he spoke to the children in the Bible some of the disciples asked the children to leave, but he rebuked them for doing this: "Leave the children alone, and don't try to keep them from coming to Me, because the kingdom of heaven is made up like this." (Matthew 19:14 HCSB)

At Christmas time when the Nativity is acted out by children it is done with such simplicity and innocence that when you see this even the hardest of hearts would be softened.

Prison
It makes you think...

Why are some of you men in prison? We need your help to build God's Kingdom. This is not the Second World War, where the women were left to take care of the land and work in the munitions factories to make the bombs. Back then it was for a good cause with the men away fighting.

The men went out to fight for freedom – the freedom that we have today. But some of you men are fighting for the wrong things and the wrong reasons. Some of you men are fighting gang, race and postcode wars leaving some women behind to deal with the fallout. Get out of the prisons you men, as Lord Kitchener once said: <u>YOUR COUNTRY NEEDS YOU</u>!

Boxing: Be the Best

In order to win a fight in the boxing ring the boxing coach will tell the person who they are training that they are to stay focused on their opponent. They are told not to look around the outside ring at family members, friends or supporters. In doing this the brain will disengage on the objective concerned and the brain will instead connect itself with what is happening outside the boxing ring. A cry of laughter or a shout from someone outside the ring could possibly distract the person who is fighting.

God does not want us to be distracted from outside influences, rather to concentrate on him as he is the metaphoric boxing ring.

When Peter walked on the water his focus was on Jesus (the metaphoric boxing ring), but when his brain became disengaged and he concerned himself with the outside things as a boxer sometimes does, he began to sink and found that he was no longer walking on the water.

"Lord, if it's you," Peter replied, "tell me to come to you on the water." "Come," he said. Then Peter got down out of the boat, walked on the water and came towards Jesus. But when he saw the wind, he was afraid and, beginning to sink, cried out, "Lord, save me." (Matthew 14: 28-30 NIV)

Preservation

We need to grasp the idea that without care and attention the things around us would decay, for example, we may take care and attention with our own personal things that are pleasing to us and that we love, but we also need to take care of the small matters first before we are entrusted with the bigger things.

When we truly care for the things of God that is when we will see him evident in our lives. The smallest of things may seem trivial to us in our lives but it is in this that we normally miss out on what God is actually saying to us. Human assumption does not account for much.

What we may see with the human eye is not what is actually happening most of the time because we may not look into the deeper things. In this life we may normally only scratch the surface of things, yet we may not look past what we cannot see. If something looks old to us we may sometimes move onto something that looks new. There is even a saying that goes, "Out with the old and in with the new," but in fact we need to hold onto the things that appear to be old, take care of them, and in return we will be rewarded by God because he is in the business of restoring lives, families, homes and so much more.

This is seen in everyday things, for instance, a person may have a bottle of wine that is perhaps 30 or 40 years old and because of the monetary benefits that it may bring it could be well kept and preserved. But the things of God may sometimes be pushed aside and not mentioned at all. God is looking for us to preserve the small things that he has entrusted to us, which are things seen as well as unseen.

It makes you think...

In the Bible (Matthew 18: 21-22) Jesus says that we are to forgive a person many times over. This requires a lot of forgiveness especially when a person has done something really bad to you or to your loved ones.

But in order to move on from certain things that may plague our lives forgiveness has to take place, because if we lean on our own strengths and understanding this would never happen, that is why I have chosen to give everything to him because I cannot do anything in my own strength. Trust in the Lord with all our heart, and do not rely on your own understanding; think about Him in all your ways, and He will guide you on the right paths. (Proverbs 3:5-6 HCSB)

Searching

When we think of birth we normally associate this with a woman giving birth to a baby. Giving birth could also mean having an idea or a dream that needs to come forth. With some births there is pain while with others it is easy depending on the situation and the coping process. Some births and ideas can be very long suffering and painful; this is called labour.

God wants us all to have an easy labour and not worry for anything. He said in his word: "Come to Me, all you who labour and are heavy laden, and I will give you rest." "Take My yoke upon you and learn from Me, for I am gentle and lowly in heart, and you will find rest for your souls." "For My yoke is easy and My burden is light." (Matthew 11: 28-30 NKJV)

He does not intend for us to have heavy burdens or hard labour but for us to have an easy life. But the fall of Adam caused mankind to labour and many to struggle in this life. When we get lost we desperately search for a way back to our base.

We may be lost on the road when we are driving or may take a wrong turn when walking down the street. That in itself is how people are with God - we take the wrong turn and end up on a different road. When we find the surroundings that we are happy and familiar with be it our home or place of work we feel that we are confident and have a safe haven.

The reason for us getting lost is to be found, because if we are not lost how can we therefore be found or find what we are looking for so that we can learn from this experience? When we are lost we are sometimes afraid or embarrassed to tell people. We feel that they may laugh at us or we may feel out of control or out of our depth.

A lot of people do not come to know Jesus for this reason, as they may feel that they may lose control of everything; this however is not the case as he doesn't rob us of things. Being lost can make us very proud and unless we are found in Jesus that is the only time when we will admit that we were lost. If we look at the parable of the lost son in the book of Luke (15:11-32) this tells us how easy it is for person to get lost and how easy it can be to be found.

Seeing is Believing

It can be said that there are some people who always like to be seen to be doing things and if they are not seen it's as if it doesn't count. In the Bible Jesus speaks about how to give without people seeing. He said: "But when you give to the poor, don't let your left hand know what the right is doing, so that your giving may be in secret. And your Father who sees in secret will reward you." (Matthew 6:3-4 HCSB)

But what we sometimes may fail to realize is that the things that are seen is sometimes less important. Some people like to be seen to be doing things on TV, or on the streets or to have stories written about them in the newspapers, but what they may fail to realize is that the things that are unseen are the most important.

When a writer delivers the final script for a TV show or a movie it is not they who is seen but the end product which is delivered on our TV screens and in the cinema.

The Bible says that we should be moved by faith and not by sight meaning that the unseen things is what really matters as God himself is unseen. So we fix our eyes not on what is seen, but on what is unseen. For what is seen is temporary, but what is unseen is eternal. (2 Corinthians 4:18 NIV)

However, in order for some people to believe they need to see some form of evidence with their own eyes. Belief and believing is basically changing your mindset and training your brain to acknowledge a substance or evidence not seen or manifested to the naked eye.

Belief, for example is faith. If you turn a tap on in your home which is marked hot water and cold water comes out instead you may be taken aback especially if you were about to get into the shower at that time. However, it should be pointed out that your mind may be programmed to expect hot water and because of this belief the expectation is high beforehand.

This is the same analogy with God working in faith. Jesus said in Matthew 7: 9-10 (NKJV), "Or what man is there among you who if his son asks for bread, will give him a stone?" "Or if he asks for a fish, will he give him a serpent?" Therefore when we have faith in receiving a particular thing we wouldn't accept something else in its place.

Never Give Up

Before you can move on or have a turning point something has to break, be it the breakdown of a relationship or friendship or the breakdown of a car (if a car is causing problems it will have to be replaced eventually). When the waters break just before a woman is about to give birth that is when she is ready to move on into the delivery process.

The Beautiful Game or is it? (Part Two)

Football players could be compared to church elders as they bring their skills to the club while the elders bring the anointing from God into the church or a ministry.

The salaries of some footballers (depending on which team they play for) can be described as vast, yet the payment an elder would receive is the anointing of the Holy Spirit, which is worth more than any financial payment.

Football supporters and the church congregation have similar traits in that some football supporters will go over and above to buy everything that is associated with the club even if they may not have much money and may make any effort possible to attend matches. In the same way some Christians may find themselves purchasing the latest book, video, DVD or audio CD so they can follow a certain teaching or message and may also go to various conferences to feel a part of the atmosphere. This type of behaviour by some Christians may make them think that they can get more from the minister rather than seeking what they can get from God instead.

Some football supporters may also look to the players and idolise or worship them for their amazing skills. It could be said that supporting a football club can at times be an expensive pursuit as some fans may set aside money to pay for their annual season ticket which helps to bring in revenue for the club, maintain the stadium and buy the best players. For those supporters who may be unable to buy a season ticket they may instead pay a subscription fee to watch their team on the various sports satellite channels. In the church Christians set aside money from their income to help maintain the church (such as to help pay the electricity, repairs to a leaking roof or other expenses).

Submission is the Key
It makes you think...

In this life we need to be able to submit to the right authority as Jesus himself knows who to submit to: his Father, who is the right authority.

True Believer (the Matchbox)

It does not matter which church you attend or what denomination you belong to in order to determine your flame/passion or to show that what you carry within you is real. It should be up to the individual person to show the light within themselves and then go on to affect the people around them. If you have a box of matches for example and you light an individual match it will be able to hold its own flame and fire. However, if the lighted match is put near the other matches in the box then the rest will light up. If a person is truly on fire for God they will ignite others around them.

Being a true believer is not just about spreading the Gospel by handing out leaflets, it is about trying to act and do the things that Jesus did. In the Bible Jesus did not just speak to his disciples and the people around him, he also showed them the love and kindness of God's Kingdom, therefore true believing Christians should be able to affect and light up things and people regardless of circumstances.

Don't hide your light! Let it shine for all; let your good deeds glow for all to see, so that they will praise your heavenly Father. (Matthew 5:15-16 TLB)

Searching

If you truly seek after something you will find it; you will research the information to help you gain further knowledge. Don't stop searching because of a situation not relating to your research, keep focusing on your goals regardless.

God's Mercy

God is merciful and his mercy endures forever; he is not a respecter of persons. I believe that with a near death experience God will speak to people as he has done on so many different occasions. God's way of thinking is different from ours and that's what makes him unique.

In the book of Matthew (20: 1-16), Jesus told the parable of the workers who went to work for a land owner and were each given a Denarius (the money used at that time) regardless of the number of hours that they had worked.

The workers that did more hours than the ones who worked for just one and two hours complained bitterly, but the landowner pointed out to them that his wages were explained before they had accepted the work.

But he answered one of them, "Friend, I am not being unfair to you. Didn't you agree to work for a Denarius? Take your pay and go. I want to give the man who was hired last the same as I gave you." (Matthew 20:13-14 NIV)

They could not argue against this as they agreed the terms before they began the work. Can you imagine if an employee at a company has given thirty years of service and a new worker arrives and within a year they receive the same pension as the person who has worked there for thirty years? How would that person feel? What an uproar that would cause.

God is not a respecter of persons. When Jesus was put on the cross, two criminals were also crucified on either side of him. One of the criminals, on realising that he might miss out on eternity asked Jesus to remember him when he returned to the Kingdom.

Then he said to Jesus, "Lord, remember me when You

come into Your kingdom." And Jesus said to him, "Assuredly, I say to you, today you will be with Me in Paradise." (Luke 23:43-43 NKJV)

In the midst of this what we see is the mercy of God, as his ways is not our ways, and he is willing to accept anyone even at the last hour.

No-entry

When we see a no-entry sign it clearly shows that we are forbidden to enter that area in question. Wherever it is shown we may ask ourselves what this means to us.

The sign speaks for itself and in our minds it means don't go there or forbidden area (such as making an illegal turn in a car, trespassing on private property or trying to illegally enter a derelict building site). At times the wrong things can spring into our minds. It's as though we are programmed automatically to do this.

In the film *see no evil, hear no evil* (1989), two innocent men are caught up in a murder, however one of the men could only hear the crime as he was blind, while the other could not hear what had taken place because he was deaf, and as a result of this the pair had entered a point of no-entry.

There are certain parts within us that are also no go areas depending on the circumstances which are the eyes, ears and mouth. They can heal, edify or empower us or on the other hand condemn, shame or kill us. It is as though we do not shield ourselves within these areas and forget that they are sometimes no go areas.

When we sometimes have a problem with someone we may say to ourselves "I won't say that to so and so as it may cause offence," yet we may still end up hurting the person if we cannot control what comes out of our mouths. The same thing should also apply when we see something with our eyes or when we hear a piece of information. We should apply the same caution and not entertain it.

The book of Proverbs warns of taking the wrong path. Before every man there lies a wide and pleasant road that seems right but ends in death. (Proverbs 14:12 TLB)

Never Give Up
It makes you think...

"Are we there yet?" is a question sometimes asked by children when they embark on a long journey. When you become of child of God, the Lord says that we are to become like little children in order to enter the Kingdom.

It is a question that is continually asked of God when we see the pain and suffering of some people on news reports or when we read about distressing news stories in the papers.

You are a child in the spirit on a journey and your goal is to reach heaven. We all have a destination to reach at some point in our lives, in fact we are faced with this everyday be it at school, work or holidays; we need to find the right direction in order to get to the right destination.

Silence

It is sometimes so easy for us to give up on things and not to pursue our dreams and goals. We need to have patience in order for things to come to pass. There is after all a time for everything. In Ecclesiastes 3:7 (NKJV) the author writes, A time to tear, and a time to sew; a time to keep silence and a time to speak.

Sometimes in the silence we can hear things that we don't want to hear, which is why most of the time we may remain busy because the truth is told to us in the silence. In the silence is where our dreams and hopes come alive - in the silence is peace and joy.

In the silence battles are won (before the regiment takes to the battlefield they remain silent in the territory so that they can receive clear instructions in order to win the fire fight and outwit the enemy).

In the silence babies are born - I was born in silence although my mother was crying and screaming while in labour. I came out in silence but when I entered the world that was when I cried.

The other element of food (the Parables) It makes you think...

Jesus spoke to his disciples in parables so that each one according to their ability was able to understand the kingdom of heaven and what was to come. Our intestines break down food in order for us to function for now and for the future. It breaks it down so that it is easy to digest. This is God – food is spirit.

I Need a Hero

The TV series *Heroes* is a good example of what God's intentions were for his people. The Bible says in the book of Genesis that we were made in the image of God.

Then God said, "Let Us make man in Our Own image, according to Our likeness..." So God created man in His own image; He created him in the image of God; He created them male and female. (1:26 & 1:27 HCSB)

Many of the characters in *Heroes* have extraordinary abilities. One character, Hiro is able to teleport and freeze time, while the artist Isaac Mendes had the ability to draw the future. God also has extraordinary abilities as he is omnipresent. Jesus' ability to walk on water was guided by God. Isaac, although having the ability to draw the future could not create it without using heroin as a substance. For Christians, Jesus is the substance that they draw from in a positive sense. While Isaac needed heroin to help create his drawings, spiritualist mediums need to rely on dead spirits to convey information to people eager to hear news relating to their things happening in their lives. The medium tries to take on the role of a superior hero - to appear to be all knowing. God however is the only one who knows everything and can see what really happens from one day to the next.

God is the hero who helps us to survive – he has the substance that we need to inject into our lives - he is the one who gives us inspiration and discernment in order to get by in life.

We're in the Army Now
It makes you think...

As soldiers for God we are instructed to love one another as it is a commandment from God to love one another. When a Major in the army gives a command the ranks follow. Love one another as you would yourself. "Do not seek revenge or bear a grudge against one of your people, but love your neighbour as yourself. I am the Lord." (Leviticus 19:18 NIV)

The Bible says that when your brother is hurting you are supposed to grieve with him and rejoice with him when he is happy. The combat situation is similar when a soldier is injured (everyone rallies round, the medic is summoned, and the wounded soldier is encouraged until they are airlifted out of that territory). Love one another and your neighbour as you would yourself.

The New Year's Honours List (synonymous to Christ) It makes you think...

The whole order of ceremonies including anointing services, baptisms and dedications is synonymous to receiving one of the Queen's Honours (MBE, OBE, CBE, Dame Hood or Knighthood). You come before royalty to receive the medal of good works. These are given for the display and compassion awarded to those who serve their society and community. When Christians come before God who has true regal status, he also gives his rewards to his children for their services and commitment to him.

You Reap What You Sow

Whatsoever a man sows he shall surely reap. From goodness come rewards and blessings. Don't be misled; remember that you can't ignore God and get away from it: a man will always reap just the kind of crop he sows! (Galatians 6:7 TLB)

From goodness comes discernment. If you are genuine you will be able to pick up whether the people around you are either for or against you, as your spirit should be able to sense an alignment together. Jesus and God with humble spirit enable them to work together. When man sows into humbleness he will reap God. Invest in him and he will invest in you and having done this you will be able to stand. When a person builds a house on sand and not on solid rock the house and their investment will come crashing down.

The Bible says, take care to live in me, and let me live in you. For a branch cannot produce fruit when severed from the vine. Nor can you be fruitful apart from me. Yes, I am the Vine; you are the branches. Whoever lives in me and I in him shall produce a large crop of fruit. For apart from me you can't do a thing. (John 15:4-5 TLB)

If you are prepared to sow into goodness you will receive goodness.

Jesus (the Manual)
It makes you think...

Follow the instructions carefully that is what the manual says. Would you know how to assemble a shelf without the manual unless you're confident that it won't fall apart?

Belief

Whatever you believe, if you put your mind to it will come to pass if you focus on the positive things; our mindset will be programmed for a positive outcome. If you believe that there is no one there for you in times of trouble then this will surely come to pass because of your strong belief in this. The mind is a powerful tool when in partnership with the mouth so we need to guard it well. When we look at things in general we don't really look closely at what is in front of us and its worth.

When we see objects say in a supermarket or a corner shop, we may only focus on the item that we are buying and not the surrounding packaging that the item is displayed on or placed in. The surrounding packaging that the item is placed in helps it to stay steady and keeps it from falling. There is someone who we cannot see and does this too. We may sometimes only focus on the thing that we think is important – the thing that we can see.

Value Brand

When we see items in a supermarket that are labelled as value brand we may see it as something that is cheap but in the thesaurus dictionary the word "value" also means excellence, worth and esteem to name but a few. When a house is burgled the person who has lost their valued possessions may say, "I've lost my valuables," therefore this tells us that what we may think or how we may see something is not how it really is. We have to look deeper into the meaning of things before we decide to brand it.

From Within

It's not what's on the outside that matters it's what's on the inside that is the real beauty, for example, a car may look beautiful on the outside but if there wasn't an engine inside it wouldn't run. The human body may look good on the outside but if the heart or the brain or other vital organs were not inside it would not function.

Let It Snow

It can be said that snow looks beautiful when it falls and covers the ground in a park or back garden. It is somewhat unspoilt and soft to touch and can be seen as beautiful to some people who are happy and amazed by its appearance, and when it falls it also mirrors the object that it falls upon clinging to its shape and form (you can see the outline of a leaf or the outline form of a bicycle by the coating of the snow).
Even the most unattractive of cars would not look out of place when covered by snow as its true appearance is concealed. When snowflakes are observed under a

microscope each patterned snow flake is similar to a doily pattern that a cake rests on. Each snowflake is different and each one is beautifully made and work together to do its job.

The Down (slide) of Snow

When snowfall occurs overnight it appears to somewhat peaceful and comes silently so you don't know when it comes, unless the weather prediction is accurate or you happen to look out of your window. When it falls on the ground or in an open space it is beautiful and when it melts it does not produce much water. But when it is contaminated with petrol and gas fumes it forms black ice on the road, which then turns to ice, becoming a hindrance and causing the roads to become slippery.

This is when the wonderful aspect of snow loses its gloss; some people can be like this too, as when the snow first falls many people are attracted to it.

We were meant to be like this in the beginning: calm and unspoilt, but man-made issues (such as lies, selfishness and hatred) have caused us to become contaminated and a hindrance; therefore we sometimes slip up and cause accidents. Some people have even been described as having an icy character about them.

Eyes Open

You will only go to the dentist if you have to because of the pain. You will only go to the doctor if you really need to. If we affect a person's life we may sometimes go with the notion of having to see this affect with our own two eyes. Although we cannot see God he affects us in more ways than we think. When a seed is planted in the ground do we constantly watch it to see it grow? It grows but we don't observe it day and night to see this as we water it and leave it to grow.

When parents see their babies open their eyes for the first time they are happy because they can now see and know the truth. When God sees us open our eyes for the first time he is happy because now he sees us and we now know the truth.

Eternal life

John 3:16 (NIV): For God so loved the world that he gave his one and only son that whoever believes in him shall not perish but have eternal life.

Unity in strength
It makes you think...

When something or a person are in unity it represents strength, for instance, if you have a rope that is made up of three strands they are usually woven together to give the rope its strength. Without the combined strands the singular strand is ineffective therefore each strand needs the other to gain strength. A mountain climber will need to have rope of a particular thickness and strength in order to carry out the expedition. The Father, Son and the Holy Spirit are one together. They represent the strands or piece of rope as all three have strength.

God's Love

God's love is genuine and pure - God's love is for everyone - God loves us even when he's rejected. When some disasters come the first one who is blamed is God. "Where was God or why didn't he stop these things?" are at times questions asked by some. But God's love is a relationship where both good and bad things happen. The sun doesn't always shine, rain also comes too. If we want things from God we have to earn his respect as well.

If you are dating someone or you are married would you expect the person who you are with to respect you if you didn't show respect to them or would you expect them just to give you things when you wanted something? You are not a fool so you wouldn't do this, neither is God a fool.

We are at War: YOUR COUNTRY NEEDS YOU!

It makes you think...

This is a message to our men both young and old: YOUR COUNTRY NEEDS YOU! You are busy waging your own battles; your gang battles, gun and knife battles and postcode battles, but do you know that this will not last forever as names come and go, buildings that are left unprotected are rebuilt and can be easily forgotten. So men, what are you really fighting for?

Angles

When you think you look okay somebody else may say that you don't. If you're going out and you want a second opinion somebody might say that you look great but you might say to yourself: "What in this old thing?" Our perspective on things will always be different because of our opinions and how we see things from another angle. A loyal friend may tell us that we're being cheated on by a loved one and that this has been going on for some time, but we may not see it from their angle as we're the one who's in the relationship, and because we are in the situation to us everything seems fine, yet it's the friend who may see the problem from the outside.

A person may look in the mirror and may not think much of themselves, but the mirror cannot show the person's true self as it only shows them from one angle, which is why when people try on a new outfit they sometimes turn from side to side to see how they look.

When a person buys a car from the showroom the salesperson will show them the interior and exterior of the car; however the car can only be seen from a certain angle. When you view it from the back you first see the car boot, back window and back tyres, but you cannot view the front of the car until you have moved round to the other side and vice versa. The same thing also applies when the car is viewed either on the right or left hand side. So who truly sees everything in only one angle?

When we look at things we have to realize that it is seen from different angles. Only God can see everything in terms of the interior and exterior of a person as nothing is hidden from him. Everything about us is bare and wide open to the all seeing eyes of our living God. Nothing can be hidden from Him to whom we must explain all that we have done. (Hebrews 4:13 TLB)

Why I believe

Belief in God is something that you get to do personally. When you are at church you may hear the message preached for about 30 or 40 minutes depending on the service that you attend, or in some cases it could take a day for the minister to deliver the message. However, it is still up to the individual to get to know God for themselves and go home and read the Word of God as well.

When you go to the doctor and you collect your prescription you go home and take the course of treatment because you believe that it's going to make you well again. If the medication is in tablet form you will have to carefully observe and follow the instructions to make sure that it is taken at the right time day and that the dosage is correct because it is your relationship now with the tablets and you know what you have to do in order to get well.

If you invest your time in God he will invest his time in you, which becomes a personal relationship between you and him.

At school or college the teachers/lecturers are like the church ministers in that they teach you the relevant subjects, but if you want to know more about the subject it is your responsibility to do more research in order to get the necessary information that you require.

This may also apply if we visit a bank or a shop and are given information from somebody who works there. Even though they provide assistance you may still require further information for your own peace of mind (such as knowing who is in charge of the services especially if you have invested time and money).

When we invest our time with God he will do likewise with us, therefore it is our job to get to know him better for ourselves by taking time to read the Word of God as well as speaking with him on a daily basis in the form of prayer, thanksgiving and worship.

The reason why I believe in God is because the people that you see every day, laugh and cry with, share secrets with, have hopes with, work with, speak to and trust are not really there for you when you really need them. I am speaking from experience. We put our trust in them, but at times they can let you down, and this can also include those who say that they have your best intentions at heart.

Would we drive a car or be a passenger in a car that doesn't have wheels? I believe in God because the things that my eyes enable me to see are not really there, which is why there must be hope in the things in which we cannot see.

There have been certain situations which have fallen

through in my life and some people have even let me down, but there is one who I do not see, one who doesn't fail me. For He Himself has said, "I will never leave you nor forsake you." (Hebrews 13:5 NKJV)

Photos

When we take a photo we have to make sure that the camera is focused correctly before we press the button. If you take an important occasion like a wedding for example, the photographer hired to take the official photographs has to make sure that their camera is focused, that they get the right lighting, and more importantly that they get all the vital shots of the bride and groom.

We need to be like this when we make a comment or give a speech because if our comments or our speech is not properly focused before we press the button (our mouths in this case) it could cause problems for us.

Instructions

An instruction for any given thing is to benefit us in our everyday lives and to guide us in the right direction. If you are given directions to put up a shelf and all the required pieces are there you would not need to add anything because you would have all that you need to assemble it.

With food, if you follow the instructions of a recipe you would carefully stick to the correct ingredients and measurements, otherwise the food could get spoiled. In a court of law people abide by the instructions of the judge regarding bail hearings, sentencing or when they are called to give evidence.

If a person follows a doctrine and decides to add on things to suit their circumstances it could spiral out of control, or if someone is taking illegal substances or prescribed drugs and they don't stick to the correct dosage as the instructions require it could have an effect on their health, and cause them to feel worse or in some cases even kill them.

If we add or take away because we feel like it and do not follow instructions it could be fatal. The Word of God is like this; we are not supposed to add on or take away anything that is written in the Bible to suit our own needs. In the book of Revelation God talks about those who add or take away from the instructions given in the Bible and the consequences that will occur because of this, therefore he is telling us that instructions are vital and important to follow.

The Beautiful Game or is it? (Part Three)

There are some football clubs that are struggling financially and may need money in order to survive, but what you may sometimes find is that some of the bigger football clubs, whose owners have vast amounts of money at their disposal may not reach out to help those in need. The smaller football clubs could be compared to some of the smaller churches in society today that are also finding it hard to stay in operation.

Some football clubs have gained a bad reputation because of a handful of people claiming to be supporters but instead go looking for trouble with rival supporters. This trouble has also led to people losing their lives because of their strong beliefs.

It can even be said that there are disputes between certain Christian denominations who believe that they are practising the correct doctrines according to Christ's word and on occasions this has led to many people dying.

Football supporters also come from all walks of life, which include working and middle class supporters to those with extremist viewpoints, and although these people come together to watch their team play it can be argued that not everybody is singing from the same hymn sheet all the time.

Many years ago when black people came to the UK in the late 50s and 60s, many found that they were not welcomed in the church and as a result went on to form their own churches. There are other problems within the church so this tells us that even in the house of the Lord there are some who do not sing from the same hymn sheet.

Unlocking Relationships

Jesus built up relationships with people first and didn't show any harshness towards the people he came into contact with. He met them at their point of need, which a lot of the time was when they desperately needed his help, and because of this they were set free of their sicknesses, diseases and personal problems. When Jesus went around healing the sick he said to some to go and tell the people of the Good News that they were healed by him while others he had healed were told not to say anything about his works.

When you unlock a safe to retrieve precious belongings or use an ATM machine to access your finances you are the only one who knows the combination or PIN numbers. When you unlock the mystery of the Gospel of Christ be aware of whom you share your testimonies with.

Shine the Light on Me

It does not matter which church you go to, how big your church is or who's preaching at your church to determine whether you are on fire for God. It is up to you as the individual to be on fire for your goals. If you take the example of a footballer, it should not depend on the club that they play for in order for them to play well with their team mates and for the supporters to get behind them.

If you light a single match it can carry its own flame/light without the help of the other matches that are in the box. But if that match were to touch the others then the whole box will come alight, so if you are the only person in your church that truly carries a flame for God then you can affect and light others that are around you. Jesus is our light and our flame. Jesus once again addressed them: I am the world's Light. No one who follows me stumbles around in the darkness. I provide plenty of light to live in. (John 8:12 the Message)

Food for Thought

This is written for whoever is young at heart. In God's eyes we are all his children and we learn new things every day, but in order to learn these things we have to go through rough times, and sometimes mess up so that we can learn from our mistakes. When this happens the truth is revealed and guidance follows.

Some young people today need people to just understand them and the certain issues that they go through. The society that we live in at present is mainly based on perfection, but not one thing can be perfect because we all make mistakes.

Young People...

There are some food items which are compatible when cooked together; they can be boiled, fried or steamed with no problems at all. Another food may however try to overpower its flavour, or could influence or discolour it when added to the pot. Young people don't be easily overpowered or influenced by somebody else.

Young People...

Leading young people at times is like leading an army through rough terrain. If the leader does not know what they are doing and has no direction then everything fails and breaks up. You always need a base to work from and have good established leaders. Take a pizza for example, it needs a base to support all the various toppings and cheese that goes on top. With good leadership and a firm base young people will achieve a great deal. Young people you need to get back to base and get back to basics!

Young People...

Be patient in all that you do as this is important. If you are cooking food and you take it off the heat before its completion it could get ruined, or if you turn up the heat in order for it to cook more quickly it could burn. Young people don't do things in haste or not at all because you think that your goals are not coming and you won't achieve them. Young people try to be careful so that you don't get burned or be held back from your achievements.

Young People...

Some young people today can sometimes find themselves under pressure from some of their peers and adults in society and it seems to be endless with gang culture and knife crime on the increase. It is fair to say that we are living in dangerous times.

If you look at carrots, parsnips and beetroots, although they are labelled as vegetables and are displayed together in the vegetable aisle of a supermarket, the beetroot if cooked together with the carrots and parsnips will end up changing the colour and appearance of the carrots and parsnips. There are also some young people who get mixed up with others and may go on to change them.

Young people you need to be careful who you mix up with as they might seem okay to hang around with because you are classed in the same group, but they may end up changing you and your character in ways that could leave you unrecognisable.

Young People...

Never under estimate what you can do as each one of you has a purpose and are capable of making a difference by still remaining the same. If you take a potato for instance it can be cooked in many different ways and still is a potato. It can be mashed or roasted, baked or fried, boiled or made into hash browns. It should also be pointed out that there are also new potatoes, which are like some young people - small but effective.

Young People...

Young people it's what counts on the inside that really matters, although it could be disguised to look good on the outside. You could have all the latest gadgets and latest trends. It could be a new car, which has a beautiful exterior, but if the inside is faulty how will that be of use to you? If you see a nice shiny apple and it looks nice on the outside only for you to find that when it is cut open or bitten into it is full of maggots what benefit is it to you? Young people it's what you can offer from the inside that really counts.

Young People...

Young girls you don't have to wear less to impress. You don't have to add a lot of paint to your face; you are lovely no matter what. Even the words in Christina Aguilera's song Beautiful say: "You are beautiful no matter what they say."

You don't have to under dress; there is a time and a place for everything. Even certain foods are covered up. Take the potato, for example, when cooked in its skin it keeps its jacket on. Some foods need to be cooked in their skins or their coverings and they still look really good, taste good and come out right.

Green bananas need to be cooked in its skin when boiled with other vegetables so it doesn't become discoloured. Young girls you don't have to discolour and show yourselves up.

Young People...

Not all foods are supposed to go together as there are some which are not compatible with each other. Young people you are the same, don't feel as though you're being left out of anything because of the pressures around you. Do carrots get upset over peas being used to complement fried cod and chips? It's just that they go better together. Young people, be careful who you get mixed up with.

Young people...

Lonely Hearts Ad: Looking for: gorgeous male or female; must be well fit; can have a laugh and be a great kisser. A lot of young people and people in general can sometimes base the above list on what keeps a relationship going, but as may you notice from the list seeking a person for a <u>loving</u>

<u>relationship</u> is not mentioned and should come first. If the above ad were ingredients for a recipe and no cooking oil or water was used before the cooking process got under way the ingredients would end up getting burnt. Young people try to make love the basis of a relationship so that hopefully you won't end up getting burned.

Young People...

When you look around there is always a pursuit happening. This may include chasing or pursuing a girlfriend or boyfriend, the latest mobile phone, clothes or iPod. Make sure that it is the right thing that you are following after otherwise the outcome might not be a good one. When you have a recipe and the ingredients are mixed together, each one has to follow in the right order for the meal to turn out right. If the ingredients don't follow in the right order the meal may end up being ruined. Young people, be careful to follow after the right things.

Young People...

Just because something looks good does not mean anything; just because a person might be good in bed does not necessarily make them a good person. A particular food may look and taste good to some but to others it might not agree with them.

Some people may have no problem with eating peanuts but for others it might affect them or could result in their death because of a bad reaction. Young people, be careful what you consume and take in just because it may look good to you.

Young People...

If you have oranges in a fruit basket and one of them goes bad you may find yourself having to throw away not only the bad one but some of the other oranges as well because they too could become affected by the rottenness of that one orange. So young people, be careful who you get mixed up with, and who you rub shoulders with.

Typecast

When a handful of people mess up whether it is a football team, teachers, church leaders or government ministers the whole group is sometimes blamed. When I was at secondary school, if someone in my class was being disruptive then the whole class would be put in detention. On a council estate if there are say maybe eighty people living in a block of flats and out of those eighty people there are four that have a character of anti-social behaviour then the whole estate is sometimes looked upon as having a bad reputation.

Photos

Memories are photos that are not physically seen but are still by a created image. It can be a place or a memory that is inside us and is triggered by so many different emotions depending on the circumstances around us.

Misgivings

In this life we may not really see the fullness of an item that we may have purchased until we have taken it home. In the film *Marley and Me* (2008), a couple go to the pet shop and buy a lovely adorable dog believing that it will enrich their lives.

Little did they know that the pet shop owner wanted to get rid of it and sold the dog to them at a cheaper price, and as the dog grows bigger it becomes more and more of a handful. Perhaps if they had known that the dog would have been too much to handle maybe they would have had second thoughts in taking it home.

You may only see the fullness of a coin once you've taken it home. When you buy something in a shop and you get back a lot of change all mixed up together, if you are in a hurry you may just put it into your purse or wallet without properly checking it. It is only when you get back home that you may realize that in the mixture of the coins you've been given some foreign currency which you may not be able to use.

I have received foreign currency as part of my change and I can tell you it is very frustrating. It's only when you purchase God for yourself and invite him into your home (by reading and understanding the Word) that you will see the fullness of God.

Memories

In the past if you heard a great song on the radio and rushed out to buy the album you may have sometimes found that there may have been only one particular song that you liked on the entire album. Fortunately, because of the digital age we now have the choice to download individual tunes.

Everything has meaning; you may for example have a favourite song, which brings about a variety of different emotions. A song may make you happy or sad and whether it does it serves its purpose and affects you. A song that may make you feel happy can hold beautiful memories like a favourite photograph. When you listen to your song you may begin to visualise your memories and when you have heard your favourite song it can somewhat make you feel as if you are looking at a photograph. When you listen to a good song you should be able to feel it.

True Exposure

When things come to light everything is exposed, for example, when a mouse or a cockroach is hiding in the dark and you put the light on it becomes exposed. If you are painting a wall and it is sunny outside the light may reflect onto the wall.

Later on when it gets dark outside and you switch the light on in the room it may show that part of the wall was not painted properly, therefore it needs to be redone.

If you are in a nightclub the lighting may make a person look different on the outside, it's only when they've left the club that their true form may be seen.

Jesus, who is the light, helps to show things for what they really are and can also guide us away from the dark spots that try to invade our lives.

Why I believe

In this life there will always be a few people who are in charge of something; there are some who may even take drastic methods to abuse their position. If you look around you will find people in charge in everyday life whether it be our place of work, government or church - it is plain to see. In this life there is someone who is in charge of everything that we cannot see.

I'm sure there's even someone in charge over many of our world leaders that the world does not see. Everything has a leader in charge of things that we can see whether it is the fire service, schools, police, army and church and if you notice we as humans haven't got the answer for everything, so there has to be someone who we cannot see and should obey as they mean serious business.

The earth is the Lord's, and all its fullness, The world and those who dwell therein. (Psalm 24:1 NKJV)

Contracts

If you have a mobile phone you may find that some phone companies may give you the option to terminate the contract when the agreement has come to an end. Whatever we do in life has a contract or agreement whether we realise it or not it has been drawn up. For example, we have a contract with our families, our spouse, our place of work and even our place of worship.

We also have a contract/covenant with God from the beginning. Before I shaped you in the womb, I knew all about you. Before you saw the light of day, I had holy plans for you: a prophet to the nations – that's what I had in mind for you. (Jeremiah 1:5 the Message)

We're in the Army Now

When a soldier goes through the basic training in the army they need to discipline and humble themselves so that they can take orders from whoever is in charge. The training can be hard and sometimes the person who is in charge of the training may use their power of authority to exploit others. There are other people who will train you without exploiting you as they are just doing their job. If a military personnel member in authority uses their position to exploit others it will eventually come to light, as nothing is hidden from the Court Marshall.

When you sign up to be a soldier for Christ you have to

discipline and humble yourself in order to take orders from others in charge. Yes, the training can be hard and sometimes the person may use their position to hurt others, but again there are some who will train you without taking advantage as they have a job to do.

If power of authority is used to exploit people then it will come to light as nothing is hidden from God.

Jesus (The Fire Fighter)

It could be said that a lot of people at times go by face value. When Jesus was amongst the people on the earth he was always questioned about his miraculous works because they didn't realise that the fire was within him. At times we may do this when we judge others. If a person is a little quiet we may say, "Oh so and so hasn't got much to say, however nobody truly knows the wealth from inside that particular person.

Even fire has an inner and an outer appearance. If you look at a forest fire for example, we can see the flames raging and the smoke rising into the air to know that danger is present and to avoid the area in question. In some cases when a house or building is on fire, you may not smell the smoke or see the flames straight away to know that danger lurks until you open the door and are beaten back by the flames.

There are all different types of talent; outward talent that is only seen on the outside and hidden talent which cannot be seen – the talent from within the hidden places. A person's profession or status does not determine their talents. I would never know the gifting in another person and someone else would never know the gifting in me. It is the fire from within a person that is important.

The Truth

Everything has to eventually show itself in its true form and identity. If a wolf is pretending to be a sheep it will eventually show its true form by the sound that it makes and when it becomes overwhelmed by the urge to kill.

If the heat is turned on in a room where the walls are not painted properly, the paint may begin to peel off the wall revealing what's behind the actual paint. There are boundaries and laws set up for us in a realm that we cannot see, therefore there is much more to this life and eventually it will show itself when the heat is really turned up.

There are some people it could be said that are unable to handle the truth. Some people may not believe in wrapping up at winter time as it is sometimes said that accessories such as hats and gloves are for wimps and it could be also seen as something to depend on.

We can also see this if we are maybe short of money. Some may see it as having to depend on somebody else and there is an old saying that goes, "I'm not a charity case, you know."

If I had an accident (say I were to break my leg and therefore could not walk, I would be assisted with a crutch until my leg is strengthened). Would I refuse help for this and hinder the chances of my leg recovering? I don't think I would refuse this. Would you?

Maturity in Christ

When we look at maturity we may measure it in terms of age or experience, but it may differ to how another person sees this as our thoughts are different from each other. A new believer of say three years could be more experienced with the understanding of God than perhaps somebody who has been a believer for most of their life. We must remember that God is not a respecter of persons, as he chooses who he sees fit and is equipped to do his work. God's ways and thoughts are not the same as ours.

It makes you think...

A list of things to do is something that reminds us of what to do and what not to do. A list is even needed for shopping. A list is needed in all things.

Dreams Do Come True

If you would just be still then you might find all that you need to know about life, but you have to seek this otherwise there is no point to it at all. All you have to do is be still and listen and you will find everything you need in order to help you find your way in this life. You may find that this already happens for some people but it could happen more so for others.

If you set out to purchase something from a shop or you may come across something that you have always wanted you will be pleased, because it is as though it has been there waiting for you and was specifically selected for you, therefore you need to have a positive mindset in everything that you do.

When you achieve this you can set out to gain anything that you want. If you set out to achieve your goals from an early age without distraction, and you stick to them no matter what anyone says, you may achieve what you set out to become. The Olympic cycling champion Sir Chris Hoy and the Formula One racing champion Lewis Hamilton both achieved their dreams to be at the top of their professions by having aspirations of success early on in their childhood. So if you want to achieve your goals just remain positive in what you do and have the mentality like that of a boxer – block out the distractions and stay focused.

Dreams come true for those who patiently wait.

Discipline

If you are a parent and your child is doing whatever they feel is best and are not listening to you would you allow this behaviour? If you have laid down ground rules and instructions and your child continues to do their own thing would you be happy with this? Love comes with instructions for protection and covering. For example, take the instructions for road safety, would you cross the road when the traffic lights are green? If man-made rules are there and are placed for a reason what about the rules and instructions that we cannot see, which are God's instructions for our lives?

Behind The Scenes

There is always something behind the scenes holding things together (if you take fine stitching for example, it holds a garment together and can only be seen when the garment is turned inside out). When medical research teams make a breakthrough in developing a new drug this takes place behind the scenes, but at times this is not recognized as we only see the medical treatment as the end result.

At times when a person is mistreated by some in the church we may see these people as being the representatives of God, therefore it is he who is blamed for the actions of some.

When a person does something well they do not always get the credit. God at times does not always get the credit for the good things as some only put the blame on him when things go wrong, but one has to remember that the reason things go wrong is because of man's distorted way of getting things done.

Voices

God's voice is heard from inspiration and from many different places, be it on the radio, in words, in colours (images) and from children. If we have people around us who can inspire us be it a teacher, politicians, campaigners, family and friends and they are mere humans, surely God can do so much more, don't you think?

When you open up your heart and your mind to the things around you then you will hear from him and you will feel it in your heart. The Bible says that the things of God will appear foolish to man and this is true as I once thought this as well when I didn't understand. If someone doesn't understand something it may appear to them as being foolish, for example, if a person speaks a different language to other people or has a thick accent, some may cruelly poke fun because they may not have the patience to try and understand what the person is saying.

When coming to know God you need to have patience and by having this is when you hear his voice and get understanding.

It's Not Our Battle

At times in this life I think that when it comes to knowledge and understanding some people at times may be all out to try and prove a point and the thing that is the focal point sometimes gets pushed aside. A child at school might be considered as a bit of a handful and the teacher may invite the parents to the school to discuss the matter face-to-face. The parents may find this revelation to be untrue and then the focus and concern about their child's behaviour might be put to one side and as a consequence may create a battle of words between the teacher and the parents.

Some boxers it can be said also talk of personal battles when holding their pre-match press conferences. Before a punch has even been thrown or swung the boxer's concern may instead turn to trying to prove a point rather than being victorious in the ring, as it has now become a personal issue if an opponent has openly or publicly disrespected them.

The book of Psalm 24:8 says that the Lord is strong and mighty in battle, therefore we do not need to worry ourselves about engaging in battles when we know who's got our back covered.

Volume

When we look at things in life we expect fullness and that is what makes us content. Examples of fullness could include having a full stomach, a great career or being full of the joy of spring. God's words holds volume because it is made up a three components: God (the creator from the beginning in the Old Testament), Jesus, (who was sent to redeem the world in the New Testament) and the Holy Spirit that dwells in and amongst his people (New Testament).

A song it could be said operates in the same way by having words, vocals and sounds. If you have someone who is struggling to speak a certain language then help in the form of an interpreter may need to be at hand so that they can understand their surroundings.

This may apply if someone needs help with a job application or having a hospital appointment and forms the basis of a three-way communication process. If you stay on the path of the Lord who created the original volume you will have clarity and understanding in whatever you do.

Spiders

Some young people it could be argued could be compared to being like spiders. If we see a spider crawling we may scream out in terror or become a gibbering wreck.

If we happen to see a group of young people together, perhaps say on a bus or walking down the street, we could assume the worse about them because we think that they are a threat. If some people see more than one spider crawling towards them they may feel threatened.

There are different types of spiders (in terms of size and shape), and this analogy could also be used to compare some young people. There are some spiders that are small and considered harmless and when they crawl about they may be just minding their own business, however because some people have a phobia about them they may be seen as frightening. In the case of some young people there are some who are harmless and just want to get on with their lives.

There is however other spiders that are very dangerous and poisonous and will entrap and kills its prey. In the same way there are also some young people who operate in a similar character by purposely setting traps for their rivals and in some cases will take their lives.

When we see a spider we may become fearful and get someone else to tackle or kill it for us, and after this has happened we may get upset especially if the spider was killed, which can be quite a strange emotion.

I think that this also happens with some young people. We may be afraid of some of them but when something tragic happens (in the event of a young person losing their life) we feel remorse. We have to remember that they are still young people, as we ourselves were also young once and sometimes made mistakes in life, therefore as adults we need to try and understand our young people and not be so quick to dismiss them.

One day children were brought to Jesus in the hope that he would lay hands on them and pray over them. The disciples shooed them off. But Jesus intervened: "Let the children alone, don't prevent them from coming to me. God's kingdom is made up of people like these." (Matthew 19: 13–15 the Message)

Behind The Scenes

There is always something behind the scenes making reality a possibility such as writing a script for a soap opera or a movie. When you see a celebrity chef on TV the food looks lovely, everything looks great but who is doing the preparation in the back behind the scenes and cleaning up at the end?

There are so many things that will make you think that there has to be a controller or an overseer behind the scenes. What about the universe, the earth and everything in it? What about the world and its inhabitants? Who is behind the scenes controlling things?

The earth and everything in it, the world and its inhabitants, belong to the Lord; for He laid its foundations on the seas and established it on the rivers. (Psalm 24: 1-2 HCSB)

Endurance

In order for something to be gained it needs to go through times of fire. A building may burn down and then many years later may be built up again and restored to look even better than its original design. In order to get work experience we may have to work at a place that we may not like in order to achieve our goals.

Gold needs to go through fire so that it can be refined and heat tested for a long period of time before it becomes metal. Diamonds in a mine are obtained by people sometimes going through pain or even risking their lives to find them. Coal miners who work deep underground have to work in tough conditions so that we can reap the benefits by having heat in our homes. Jesus died on the cross so that we can have a better life from his pain.

Stop and Think

When we are waiting for something to happen it can sometimes be quite a wait, it might be waiting for a bus or maybe waiting for some important news to arrive. When perhaps we have misplaced something, it is only when we stop looking for it and then try to think where we have placed it that we may stumble across it.

Cleansing

There is a well-known cleaning substance that is put into the washing machine in order to make it run properly. It cleans up the machine so that it does not clog up with limescale. If excessive limescale is built up it could up damaging the inside of the machine. We need to look after our own bodies by feeding ourselves the right foods, drinking the right liquids and taking the right medication so that our bodies don't clog up.

Care and Attention

When a plant is watered and looked after it will grow, if it is not watered properly it will die. A computer needs to be installed with the right software in order for it to work. If you drive a car that runs on diesel would you put petrol in it? Make sure that the right knowledge is installed in you.

Where were you when I needed you?

Sometimes when illness affects someone who is a Christian and believer in God it can be hard as some people around them may ask: "How come that person has died, why didn't God show up for them or why did God allow them to become ill?"

The Bible says that when Jesus' friend Lazarus was unwell, Mary and Martha invited Jesus to visit their brother. Jesus on being asked to visit arrived late and in that time Lazarus had died. The people around him again questioned why he could not save his friend who was dear to him as he had saved many others. However, when Jesus called Lazarus to come forth from the tomb he awoke up and came out. When Jesus was crucified the people that were gathered and who passed by the cross also questioned whether he was the son of God and that if he was, why then could he not save himself from death.

God will intervene in situations that are not to our understanding in order for his glory to be seen. Without pains and illnesses how can a miracle be seen whether it be a medical miracle or a worldwide phenomenon? As he went along, he saw a man blind from birth. His disciples asked him, "Rabbi, who sinned, this man or his parents, that he was born blind?" "Neither this man nor his parents sinned," said Jesus, "but this happened so that the work of God might be displayed in his life. (John 9:1-3 NIV)

Volume

The rubber, air and the metal framework in the middle make up the components of a tyre for a vehicle - without each other it cannot operate. When we look at it we may only see the tyre as the finished product. When a vehicle has done many miles on a rough road, after time the tyres need air to be put into it in order to keep the vehicle moving and to prevent it from getting a flat tyre.

God, Jesus and the Holy Spirit (as the Trinity) operate in a similar manner to keep things moving. The Holy Spirit is the air which operates in a believer - without it they too may become flat.

Strongholds

Strongholds controlling strongholds could be likened to having toothache. It may take a lot of drilling and intensive cleaning to get deep down to get to the root of the problem and the process can also be painful. The Bible says in 2 Corinthians10: 4 (NIV): The weapons we fight with are not the weapons of the world. On the contrary, they have divine power to demolish.

It makes you think...
Only the lowly

We are all lowly depending on how we may look at things in terms of our status and careers because we truly do not have what we possess.

Peace

Peace is something that can seen and felt in the right situation. If a country seems to be at peace, you may not be able to see it unless you go to that country and experience its peacefulness firsthand. When something seems calm and okay in life it could change very quickly. All may seem perfect and peaceful, but in reality it may change because what we sometimes see is not how it really is. True peace comes from God; we cannot see him but we will feel a peace when we truly know him.

Building Relationships

Some people believe that when you do something for them they do not have to contact or thank you for what you have done. Some people may think that they can just pick up the phone and ask for a favour without having to build up a relationship or friendship. Perhaps you were asked to help out at a function and after you had offered your services you may find that the person who asked the favour has gone AWOL. After a year or so the person may contact you out of the blue with that classic saying, "Oh, I was just thinking about you," and will see nothing wrong in not keeping in touch.

Christ wants us to build relationships, as he builds up relationships with people, not because he needs or wants anything from us but because he truly wants to be in our lives.

Poem about Air

In this life we often look to see if we have affected something by having to see it with our own eyes in order for us to believe it to be real.

We cannot see air, but it is there
We feel it in the air, this air
Air in the tyres, air con in the cars
Air in the sky and moving through the stars
Airy fairy stories that we were told not to believe in
But air is here now as it was in the beginning
If you plant a seed would you stay up all night without sleep to watch it grow?

Accountability

Just because you may be in charge of something big such as running an institute does not mean that you are above the law. In this life we are all accountable to
someone whether it is our parents, brother, sister or guardian. So then, each of us will give an account of himself to God. (Romans 14:12 HCSB)

Injustice

When someone commits an act of wickedness or injustice against another person, in some cases it is the victim who gets the blame. If a person owes you money or has taken something from you and won't return it you may find yourself having to chase that person only to be ignored, and at times you may be made to feel guilty because of their actions. Say for example an intruder comes into your home, to protect yourself you may use a weapon against them, but instead you could find yourself being arrested or convicted because of their wrong doing.

When things happen in some churches with a handful of people doing all manner of things not pleasing in God's sight it is God who is blamed. Jesus was told that he was not the son of God by his accusers and was blamed for many wrong doings but he was guiltless.

When he went to the cross guilt was put upon him for something that he did not do. The book of Isaiah 53:5 says that Jesus took on the guilt and the sin of the people but he was blameless in God's sight. Many people in this society may make some feel guilty for the things they have done but God sees everything.

The Right Source of Life

When our mobile phone battery is low we get the charger to recharge it so that it is replenished and can function properly. Even a phone needs a source of life to work. You may find that a particular phone brand needs its own charger and cannot use just any phone charger as it will not fit and therefore will not work. What we see here is that it is impossible to use a mobile phone without using the correct charger, which metaphorically means that you cannot go through Jesus unless you go through the correct method which is the father. "Jesus told him, "I am the way – yes, and the truth and the life. No one can get to the Father except by means of me. (John 14:6 TLB)

Communication (the Right Way)

Everything has a way of communicating whether it is the birds tweeting or rabbits stamping their hind legs, having the ability to understand Braille, sign language or lip reading – communication does not have to be always carried out in spoken form.

If a person is deaf there is a way to communicate with them provided the right training is given. When God speaks to people they are able to understand him with the right training.

Why then it is hard for us to ignore the little things that could end up causing us harm or lead some of us to even kill? We need to learn how to cope with the small things and issues and keep them small. With gangs and youth crime it maybe something small that triggers an argument and the whole situation then gets out of control.

When we put water into a filter it cleans out the impurities and is good for us. If we receive nuisance phone calls it becomes something of an irritation, because the person on the other end of the line is playing mind games by not answering when you say hello, or is making heavy breathing sounds. It is interesting that although we may get angry we have no choice but to learn to channel our anger because we cannot see them face-to-face. We need to learn how to get rid of negative influences in a non- violent way.

God/Jesus = CCTV

A nightclub bouncer or a door man can get a person into a club and can have them thrown out of a club. He is usually very strong in build and stands by the door, and if it's a private party and your name is not down on the guest list then you won't be going in. He has the control to choose who he sees fit to come in and can sometimes judge a clubber by the clothes that they are wearing as to whether they are suitable to enter. He sometimes wears an ear piece to relay information back to staff inside the club if there is any trouble so that the matter can be swiftly sorted out.

He has to remain alert at all times and keep an eye on people who are up to no good by watching their every move. Some clubs have CCTV which also keeps a watch on people and will show up any suspicious activity. God is like the door man as he has the final say as to who gets into his club (heaven), and he can also have you put you out if your name is not down on the list.

The Beautiful Game or is it? (Part Four)

Some Christians may go to church regardless of the weather conditions and in some cases some football fans may also do this. Some football fans may travel hundreds or thousands of miles just to see a match, while some Christians may even travel abroad to hear the Word of God. We can also see comparisons between the Bible and football shirts. It is very likely that you will come across a football shirt on sale somewhere in the world, whether it is purchased in the club shop or bought from a market stall.

With the Bible it can be said that there will always be a copy in print somewhere around the world and comes in many different versions. When you look at a football shirt there are many different styles going through the years to this present day, and even in the remotest parts of the world you will find people wearing them. Football is played where unity abounds and when the team is winning. This analogy also applies to the church – unity abounds when everybody is in unity.

The Unshakable Tree

When birds build their nests to dwell in they gather together the strongest material to build it. When you see a bird's nest in a tree on a windy day the wind is beating the nest in the tree but because it is so secure it doesn't fall out. The birds go about their daily business and when they return the nest is still intact. They have built it on the solid rock foundation of the tree that cannot be shaken.

The True Servant

He said: "Just as the Son of man did not come to be served, but to serve, and to give His life - a ransom for many." (Matthew 20:28 HCSB) Jesus came to heal the sick, heal the broken hearted, declare liberty to the poor and set the captives free.

Animals

Animals it can be said are in tune with what is happening on the earth and although they cannot talk there is a way of communicating with us humans, as they are very intelligent. Certain animals will know when there is a storm coming, can sense danger and are able to alert other animals and humans (if there is a fire the animal may be able to rouse their owner) in order to have an escape route.

Animals also contribute a lot to society. They can be seen as a friend and a comforter to many people who are unwell or are hospitalised and going through the recuperation process. They can also assist humans in jobs such as police border control, the army and search and rescue operations. They are also household pets and are even used in TV programmes, advertisement campaigns and films.

Dogs are also trained to assist those who are blind; animals also feel emotions in that they have the same illnesses as humans such as arthritis, cancer and diabetes.

They were created for a purpose and should be highly valued. Ecclesiastes 3:19 says that man and animal both breath the same air and both die, therefore mankind has no real advantage over these animals.

There can be only One

It is only when you know God deep down that you can then cast aside or forget about the people who have hurt you - you now come to the realization that God is the only one to focus on. To be more precise, he is the only one that will be there after everything has passed away. Jobs, businesses, people and relationships all come and go as they only exist for a short while. Heaven and earth will pass away, but My words will never pass away. (Matthew 24:35 HCSB)

Lest We Forget

With life experiences there needs to be a good level of communication in order to bring about togetherness and understanding. If a company no longer exists or if some people leave a company having spent many years of service there, you may find that the knowledge and experience goes with them. A recipe that has been handed down from generation to generation brings knowledge to the person who has received it because of its preservation over the years.

We have recently said goodbye to the last surviving men who resided in the UK and fought in the First World War, however, their testimonies of the war firsthand brings knowledge to those who may not truly understand the importance of what it means to fight for freedom and country. That is why it is important to know about the past so that we can learn for the future.

Say for instance new workers employed in a company didn't gain the right experience about the company's foundations from more skilled workers, what you might find is that some companies may not survive as they could lack the knowledge to move forward and remain competitive.

The Bible says in Matthew 24:35 (NKJV), Heaven and earth will pass away, but My words will by no means pass away.

Right Methods

When you are dealing with spiritual things they need to be dealt with in prayer, otherwise you could be searching for the wrong methods and in doing this you could go by your own understanding, which could result in going against the grain and damaging yourself in the process of finding the right method.

In order to follow the right methods you need to sharpen your mind with the right tools. If you are cutting a joint of meat for instance it needs to be cut on the right side of the grain, otherwise it may become difficult to cut. If you are using a knife to cut something it needs to be sharpened with the right tools in order to get a cleaner cut. If you don't sharpen a knife with the necessary tools you could end up cutting yourself because of the bluntness of the knife blade, which may cause the cut to be more painful. Remember to sharpen your mind with the right tools.

Baggage

A relationship is a journey in which two people travel together; therefore they need to be on one accord to understand each other. If one person is going through an issue, what you may sometimes find is that they could inflict their issues onto the other person making the journey for both of them become more difficult.

Some people may even be unaware of this in terms of what they are doing to the next person. The Bible speaks about mixing with and being edified by the right people and also tells us to offload our baggage onto Jesus. With some relationships it can be said that it is sometimes not fair for one person to offload their baggage onto the next person as someone will end up paying for it.

If you go on holiday and you check your baggage in at the airport you will find that there are even restrictions in place as to the amount of baggage you are allowed to take on the plane. If there are two people travelling together and the baggage restriction exceeds the required amount it may end up costing one person, or if they cannot pay the other person may have to pay instead.

Either way it could cost both people in terms of payment or having to leave items behind. The Bible says Come to Me, all of you who are weary and burdened, and I will give you rest. (Matthew 11:28 HCSB)

Words

It's amazing that every word in the dictionary has a particular definition that could either have a positive or a negative effect. Words are interesting in that they have different meanings for different situations or circumstances. Some words are used more often while some are hardly used at all. The words "shallow" and "deep" is interesting because if you find yourself in the deep end of a swimming pool then caution should be applied, especially if you are not a strong swimmer, therefore you would tend to avoid it and go to the shallow end which would seem a safer option.

If we are talking with someone we may say, "That conversation was deep," as we could be intrigued by the conversation because of the depth and meaning. If a person comes across as being thoughtless they could be called shallow and we may distance ourselves from them.

God All By Himself

God is everlasting and although this heaven and earth will pass away not one drop of his word will pass away. People come to know him for whatever reasons and it is a relationship which cannot be broken. He never leaves or forsakes his people and the people that are called to him cannot be taken from his hand. The Bible says that he will never forsake us, but what you may sometimes find is that people may forsake him for whatever reason they have. God however is a forgiving God as there is no-one else that forgives like him.

The Beautiful Game or is it? (Part Five)

In football competitions like the World Cup you can find yourself getting caught up in the atmosphere if you happen to be watching a pulsating game. In church you may find yourself cheering or shouting during worship music. If however there is a lack of atmosphere in the church this could make some people lose interest. Some football fans have also been criticised for not being vocal enough when getting behind their team or stirring them to victory, therefore the atmosphere in the football ground becomes artificial.

You can also hear in the football grounds chants by supporters, which have been inspired by familiar Christian hymns along the years and the words have been substituted for their own needs, so although many may substitute religious values for football in their lives, it is worth remembering that EVERYTHING IN THIS WORLD IS GOD INSPIRED!

Time

It's interesting to see how words or events which have happened in our lives make us either embrace or disregard it. If we have taken a relaxing holiday and have enjoyed the time away we may not want it to end and instead want the time to go slow. If we're searching the internet and we want information in a hurry we may purchase broadband connection in order to speed things up.

A child at school may want the day to go slow or the day to speed up depending on how they are feeling. When we are with people who we appreciate we may want the time spent with them to go slow. There is a time and a season for everything; there is a time to move fast and a time to slow down. We have choices in all that we do.

Jesus the Central Line

There are so many different phone, electric and gas companies claiming to offer different deals and packages at a cheaper price so that we may choose to become a customer with them. When we are presented with these offers we may leave the original company that we were with in order to go over to the company offering us the better deal. After some months later, although things may seem cheaper early on and you appear to be getting a reasonable deal you are still connected to the main line or source that you left, so what you may find is that you should have perhaps stayed with the original company in the beginning.

If you take the phone industry, customers have to pay line rental usage to a well-known phone company even though they might be with another telephone provider.Our reason for leaving the original company is that they may have been too expensive and the other company who you went over to provided a better deal.

When travelling on the London Underground, the Central Line is the line that connects up to many different stations on the tube network and provides a frequent travel service for passengers.

When serving the Lord Jesus Christ, for some people it could be seen as costly as they could be made to feel that they may have to give up the things which are dear to them in order to follow him. However, what we have to remember is this, when we choose a cheaper company because of the great packages that they provide what you'll find along the way is that they are still using the original source (which is the main supplier), no matter what name it now decides to call itself.

Communication

Before I became a Christian I would laugh at people who spoke to me about the Lord. I remember at one particular workplace where a former colleague and I would laugh about a fellow worker who witnessed to us. I was 18 at the time and used to smoke and during my cigarette breaks this person would irritate me badly. She would come up to me and say, "Tracey, why are you smoking? Jesus doesn't want you to smoke." To which I turned to her and replied sarcastically "Firstly, what has it got to do with you and secondly, what has it got to do with him?"

I found this colleague to be weird in terms of the things that she said and my other colleague and I would laugh and say that we weren't interested in hearing about the Gospel. But even when we laughed and poked fun at her she never got angry and remained calm. She even said to us on one occasion that the Lord loves us and that he would speak to us eventually. Although it seems like it happened yesterday I now understand what she was saying all those years ago.

When I went to Sunday school I never really understood the fullness of God. Perhaps it was the way in which the Bible was explained by the minister, I really don't know, but as I got older, I eventually realized that I had to go away and find out about Jesus for myself.

It could be said that some people during their childhood may have created an imaginary friend who they could not see but would communicate with them. This could have come about because some children might have felt that they were misunderstood by others or to escape bullies they would create someone that would always be there for them and would protect them in times of trouble.

Christians communicate with God in many different ways, although he is not seen. This variation of communication could depend on the person, their circumstances and background.

The Bible says in Acts chapter 9 that Saul was on his way to Damascus to persecute Christians as it was his job to round them up and while travelling on the road to Damascus he was temporarily blinded. When this happened the Bible tells us that Saul heard a voice and the people who were travelling with him only saw light, but did not hear the voice, therefore God communicated with Saul in a way that only he heard and knew that the Lord spoke directly to him.

If you are a parent and you have three children for instance your ways in communicating with each child may be different. With one child you may have to keep talking and saying the same thing over and over again in order for them to listen to you. With another child all it may take is a stern look for the child to know that you mean business, while to another child you may not need to say anything at all. God communicates to his children in many different ways and only the individual will know if they are willing to listen to him.

I've Created a Monster
It makes you think...

The bendy bus could be compared to Frankenstein's monster. It was an idea taken from different parts of the world, as was Frankenstein's monster which was made up of different body parts. They both seemed like a good idea at the time but in truth end up costing dearly. Why create something which you cannot handle?

Marmite

One man's loss is another man's gain because to one person a certain thought or possession may seem to be useless yet to another it's a jewel. A school teacher who is liked by one child may be seen in a different perspective by another.Unwanted clothes given to a charity shop by one person could be designer wear for another.

A relationship or friendship that ends badly could be joy for another because they see the person differently. Jesus lost his life in order for us to gain ours and in many ways people either loved him or hated him, which was evident when he inhabited his earthly body, and this love and hatred for him continues still to this day.

The Man Who Can't Be Moved

The man who has everything is seen in some people's eyes as having nothing
The man who didn't complain about how he was treated and yet took on everyone's burdens and problems
The man who is full of wisdom and power is seen by some as a joke
The man who when you and I die will still be talked about
The man who can't be moved is Jesus Christ

Numbers

Our lives it could be said could perhaps be more effective and rewarding if we are able to touch the life of just one person rather than trying to affect the lives of maybe ten people. When Jesus told the parable of the lost sheep, even though ninety nine were still at hand, the focus and importance turned to not giving up on the one sheep that was missing.

Sometimes when we try to take on many things it can become a struggle therefore we may have to sometimes concentrate on one thing at a time. Then Jesus told them this parable: "Suppose one of you has a hundred sheep and loses one of them. Does he not leave the ninety-nine in open country and go after the lost sheep until he finds it?" (Luke 15:3-4 NIV)

God/Superman

When you're trying to save someone you have to make sure that your own back is covered. The original *Superman* (1978) film starring the late Christopher Reeve is
very interesting. In one scene when Superman comes to the rescue of the heroine Lois Lane and saves her from falling to her death, she looks at him and is surprised that they are flying together and says to him: "You've got me, who's got you?"

Who has truly got you in times of trouble? God is our refuge and strength, a helper who is always found in times of trouble. (Psalm 46:1 HCSB)

Fashion

If the church is seen to be outdated what say fashion? Does that not come round full circle again be it the Ra-Ra skirt, Rubix Cube or pick "n" mix sweets? Sooner or later Jesus will be the only one who will remain in fashion because he will be the only one left to follow as all the other fashion trends will fade away.

Water

When we look at water it can be pure and also cleansing depending on the source where we get it from. Water is needed for washing, to cleanse our bodies as well as cleansing the earth (if the earth becomes too hot then water is needed for it to cool down).

When Jesus met the Samaritan woman at the well he asked her for a drink as he was thirsty. The woman was surprised by this request because Jews and Samaritans did not get along.

Jesus offered her living water that would not run out, as he is the life source: The water which doesn't run out.

"But whoever drinks from the water that I will give him will never get thirsty again – ever! In fact, the water I will give him will become a well of water springing up within him for eternal life." (John 4:14 HCSB)

Gentleness

If you go out to preach the Gospel or tell people about the Lord you have to make sure that you go out with the spirit of truth, gentleness, love, and a humble nature. It would be unwise to hammer the Gospel down the people's throat as the Lord sees and hears everything. When we read about Jesus befriending people in the Bible we see that he built up relationships with them first and spoke with them in a gentle manner.

We need to do this because if we don't we could find ourselves falling flat on our faces. If you ride a bike you would do this sensibly to make sure that you would be fine. If you don't take your time and abruptly hit the brakes, you could find yourself falling flat on your face.

The Choice is yours

You cannot help a person who does not want to be helped - it's their choice. There is a saying that goes: "You can lead a horse to water but you cannot make it drink." A lot of the healing which took place in the Bible came about by the positive belief of some of the people that Jesus made them well. The books of Matthew and Luke write about the woman with the issue of blood. She had been ill for twelve years, and we can assume that she spent a considerable amount of time and money in trying to get well.

It is also a process that still happens in this present day if we are not well. If we have the finances we may resort to seeking private treatment that could cure us of whatever complaint we have.

As Jesus was passing with his disciples the woman was so determined to be healed that she said to herself: "If only I may touch His garment, I shall be made well." (Matthew 9:21 NKJV)

When she touched his garment, Jesus realised that power had left him and on recognising this he turned round and said to the woman: "Be of good cheer, daughter, your faith has made you well." And the woman was made well from that hour. (Matthew 9:22 NKJV)

So if you need help, regardless of your circumstances, you need to believe that it will come to pass.

Poem about Death

Death, what are you doing here today?
You're early. I was not expecting you this today
Could you come back tomorrow, I'm busy, so could you delay my death as I cannot pay
Tomorrow would be better as I will have everything ready and prepared that day
The day after people will be able to shed their tears for me and then I will have no more fears
Come back tomorrow, please I beg you this day
Come back tomorrow for your pay
For today, this day, all I want to do is pray

The Death Collector

Death comes to us all. It is not a respecter of person, colour, gender, age, appearance, wealth or influence; it is something that we cannot escape. You might be able to avoid someone you may not like by pretending you've not seen them or cross the road to avoid them, but with death it is something that shows up and we cannot avoid it. Death is a part of life and vice versa and it is something that only you go through and have to deal with at the end. If a person for instance is on their death bed, although they may be surrounded by their loved ones it is still a thing that the person endures on their own.

Death shows up either at the right or the wrong time for some people, but it is something that shows up regardless. There are some people in this life who are trying to remain forever young by undergoing cosmetic procedures, but we must remember that it's only the outward appearance that is being changed here, the inward appearance is still decaying and no matter how great a person may look on the outside death still comes to them.

It should also be pointed out that even an organ transplant to save a person's life may not result in a prolonged life as sometimes the organ could be incompatible with the person receiving it. Death is not a respecter of person, colour, gender, age, appearance, wealth or influence.

Life

Life is something that you face alone - it is a journey. Even when you are born it is only you who is pushing your way out to enter the world. If you're a twin you don't both come into the world together at the same time unless you're conjoined, one will come out before the other and the gap between this could be a few minutes or a few hours later. Life is not a respecter of person, colour, gender, age, appearance, wealth or influence.

Eternal life

John 3:16: For God so loved the world that he gave his one and only son that whoever believes in him shall not perish but have eternal life. (NIV)

Bible Versions

HCSB Holman Christian Standard Bible

TM The Message

NIV New International Version

NKJV New King James Version

TLB The Living Bible

Lightning Source UK Ltd.
Milton Keynes UK
UKOW03f1856230514

232232UK00001B/3/P